THE
TAROT
COLORING BOOK

THE TAROT COLORING BOOK

PETER GRAY

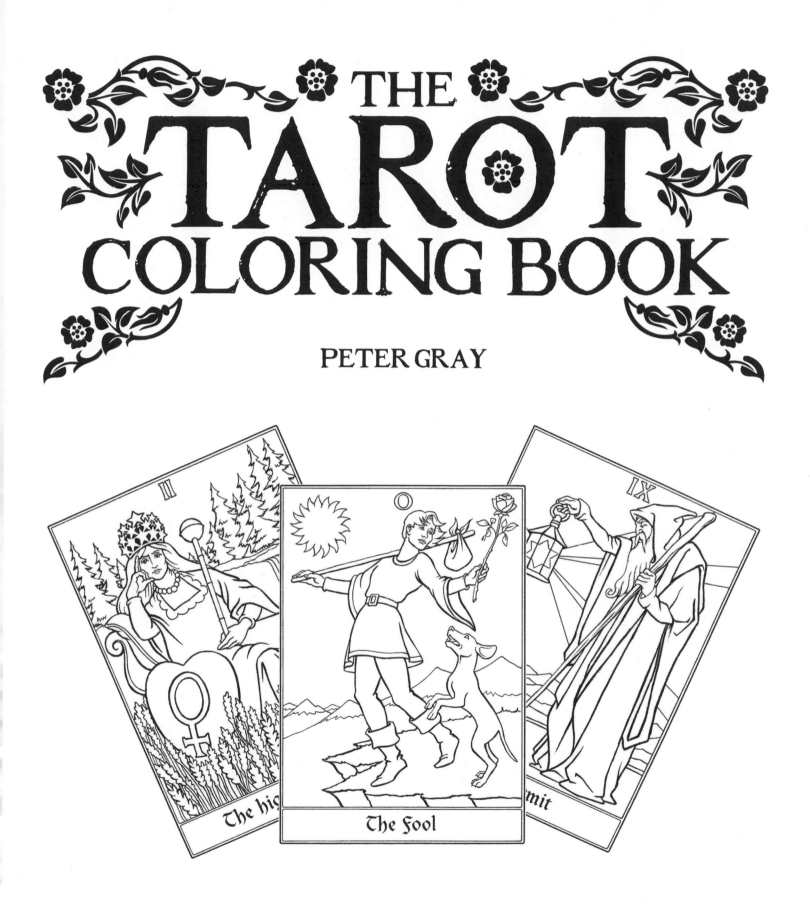

The Fool

 SIRIUS

SIRIUS

This edition published in 2021 by Sirius Publishing, a division of
Arcturus Publishing Limited,
26/27 Bickels Yard, 151–153 Bermondsey Street,
London SE1 3HA

ISBN: 978-1-3988-1445-5
CH010158NT
Supplier 29, Date 0921, Print run 11851

Printed in China

Introduction

Tarot cards have been in use since the 15th century. They were originally created for playing games such as tarocchini in Italy and, indeed, the name "Tarot" derives from the Italian word *tarocchi*. It was only in the 18th century that these cards started being used for the purposes of divination.

Over time, artists have created wonderful sets of cards with some beautiful and often highly detailed images. The set presented in the following pages offers coloring enthusiasts the chance to appreciate the characters and objects associated with the Tarot as well as some additional images that are sympathetic to the mystical nature of the cards.

Whether you are interested in Tarot itself, or simply intrigued by the delightful artwork, by completing the images within, you will enjoy many pleasurable hours of coloring.

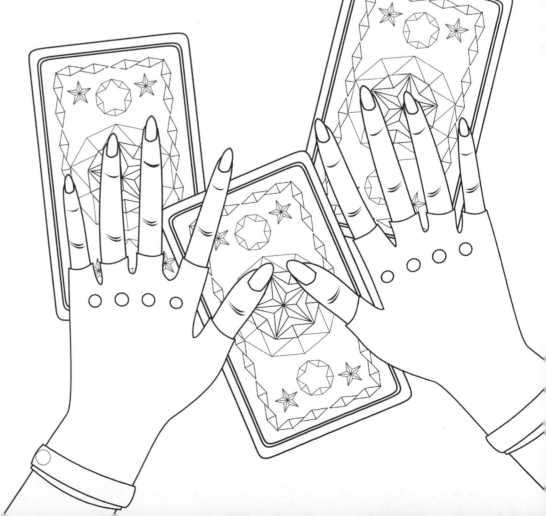

The Fool

The Magician

The High Priestess

The Empress

The Hierophant

The Emperor

The Lovers

The Chariot

Strength

The Hermit

Justice

Wheel of Fortune

The Hanged Man

Death

The Devil

Temperance

The Tower

The Star

The Sun

The Moon

Judgement

The World

2 of Wands

Ace of Wands

3 of Wands

4 of Wands

6 of Wands

5 of Wands

7 of Wands

8 of Wands

9 of Wands

10 of Wands

Knight of Wands

Page of Wands

Queen of Wands

King of Wands

Ace of Cups

2 of Cups

3 of Cups

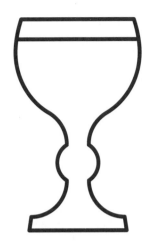

4 of Cups

6 of Cups

5 of Cups

7 of Cups

8 of Cups

9 of Cups

10 of Cups

Knight of Cups

Page of Cups

Queen of Cups

King of Cups

2 of Swords

Ace of Swords

3 of Swords

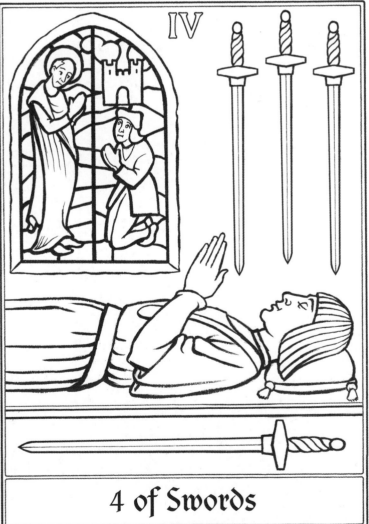

4 of Swords

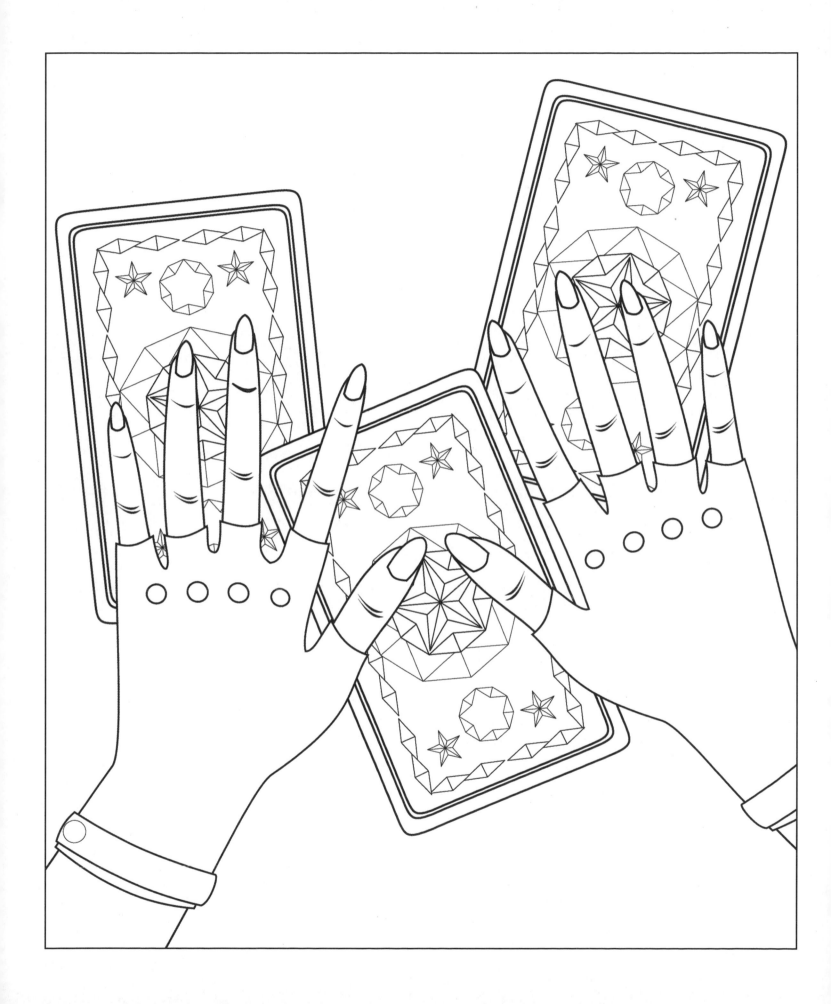

VI

6 of Swords

V

5 of Swords

7 of Swords

8 of Swords

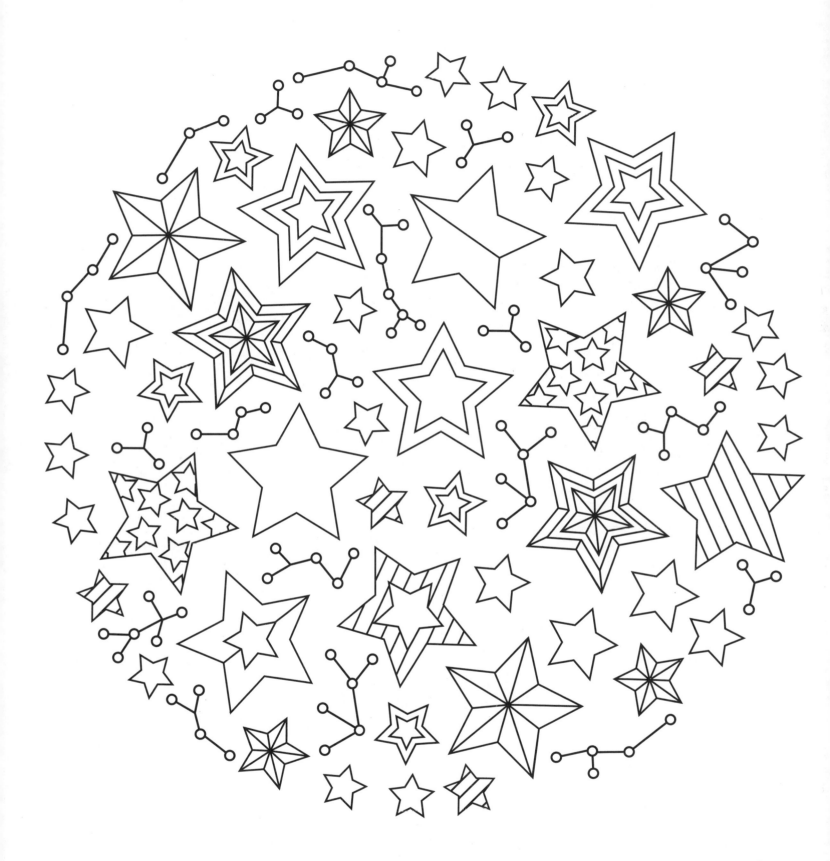

10 of Swords

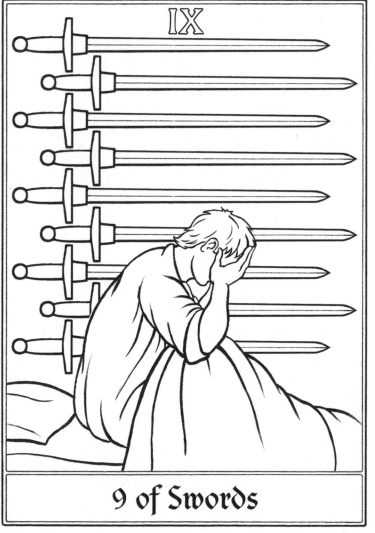

9 of Swords

Page of Swords

Knight of Swords

Queen of Swords

King of Swords

Ace of Coins

2 of Coins

4 of Coins

3 of Coins

5 of Coins

6 of Coins

8 of Coins

7 of Coins

9 of Coins

10 of Coins

Page of Coins

Knight of Coins

Queen of Coins

King of Coins